American Revolution

written and illustrated by
Rod Espinosa

visit us at
www.abdopublishing.com

Published by Magic Wagon, a division of the ABDO Publishing Group, 8000 West 78th Street, Edina, Minnesota 55439. Copyright © 2009 by Abdo Consulting Group, Inc. International copyrights reserved in all countries. All rights reserved. No part of this book may be reproduced in any form without written permission from the publisher.
Graphic Planet™ is a trademark and logo of Magic Wagon.

Printed in the United States.

Written by Rod Espinosa
Illustrated by Rod Espinosa
Edited by Stephanie Hedlund and Rochelle Baltzer
Interior layout and design by Antarctic Press
Cover art by Rod Espinosa
Cover design by Neil Klinepier

Library of Congress Cataloging-in-Publication Data

Espinosa, Rod.
  American Revolution / written and illustrated by Rod Espinosa.
    p. cm.
  ISBN 978-1-60270-179-3
  1. United States--History--Revolution, 1775-1783--Juvenile literature. I. Title.

  E208.E79 2009
  973.3--dc22
                        2007051626

TABLE of CONTENTS

Timeline..4

Chapter 1
America Discovered.............................6

Chapter 2
The French and Indian War.................8

Chapter 3
Rise of the Patriots.........................12

Chapter 4
The First Continental Congress........16

Chapter 5
The War for Independence.................20

Chapter 6
The Hardships of Revolution.............23

Chapter 7
An Eagle Is Born..............................26

Glossary...31

Web Sites...31

Index...32

Timeline

1754 to 1763 - The French and Indian War was fought.

1764 to 1767 - Great Britain taxed the colonies to pay for the French and Indian War with the Sugar Act, the Stamp Act, and the Townshend Act.

1770 - British troops fired into a crowd and killed five men during the Boston Massacre.

1773 - Colonists rebelled by dumping British tea in Boston Harbor during the Boston Tea Party.

1774 - The First Continental Congress met in Philadelphia.

1775 - The Battle of Lexington and Concord started the Revolutionary War; the Second Continental Congress met in Philadelphia.

1776 - On July 4, the Declaration of Independence was adopted; the Declaration was signed on August 2.

1775 to 1783 - The Revolutionary War was fought.

1781 - Cornwallis surrendered to Washington at Yorktown; battles continued during peace talks.

1783 - British troops left New York.

1787 - The U.S. Constitution was ratified.

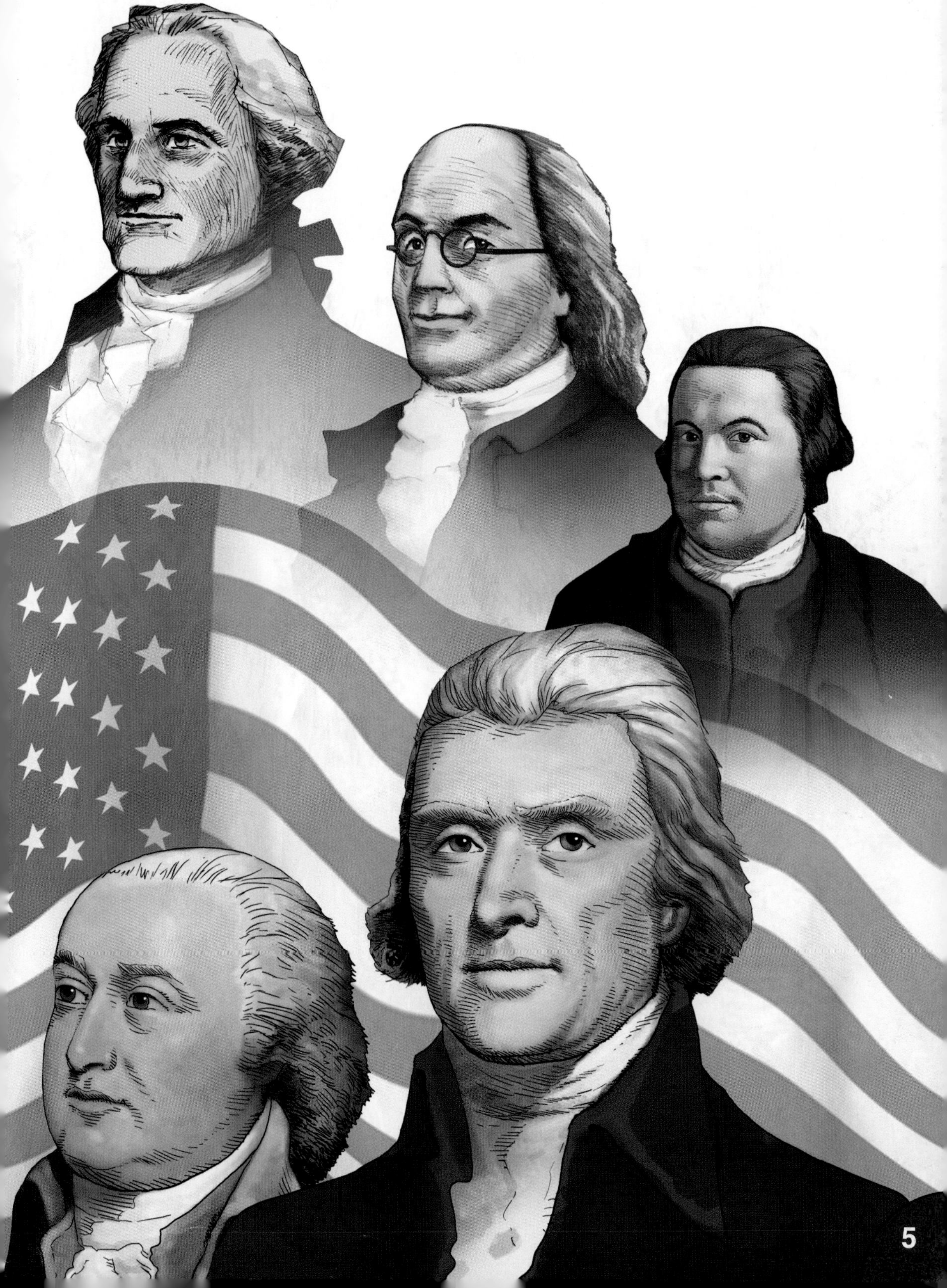

In 1492, Spanish explorers landed in America.

Christopher Columbus was the first European to set foot in the New World.

WHAT A BEAUTIFUL PARADISE.

WHO KNEW SUCH A WORLD EXISTED WEST OF THE GREAT OCEAN?

They did find gold. And where there was wealth to be made, other maritime powers came. Great Britain and France took control of the north. Spain held the southern part of the continent.

Chapter 2 — The French and Indian War

At the start of the 1700s, America was a land of opportunity. Trade flourished in New England.

WAR WITH FRANCE IS COMING. WHAT DOES HIS MAJESTY COMMAND, GOVERNOR?

WE'LL GATHER VOLUNTEERS AND USE THEM AGAINST THE FRENCH.

England had control of the seas. This made it a very powerful country. England also had a huge army. The British soldiers were called "redcoats."

Conflicts soon arose. England and France began fighting over territories.

The English raised an army to fight France.

JOIN US AND DEFEND YOUR HOMES AGAINST THE FRENCH OPPRESSORS!

BUT WE TRADE PEACEFULLY WITH THE FRENCH IN QUEBEC.

WE EXPECT YOU TO BE LOYAL TO KING GEORGE.

The French and Indian War lasted from 1754 to 1763. England and the colonists fought against France and its Native American allies.

England was victorious. The Treaty of Paris was enacted in 1763. It banished France from North America forever.

THREE CHEERS FOR HIS MAJESTY'S ARMY!

Victory after victory followed for England. One of the greatest victories was the defeat of the Marquis de Montcalm at Quebec by 32-year-old general James Wolfe.

The American colonists were happy and content once again to conduct business and trade. It was a good time to be a British colonial citizen.

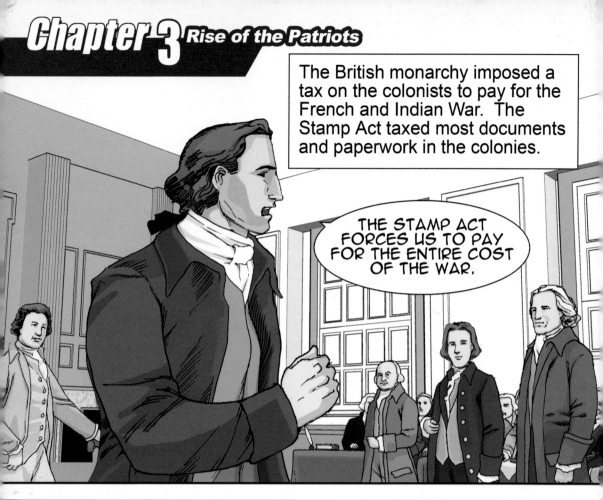

The British monarchy imposed a tax on the colonists to pay for the French and Indian War. The Stamp Act taxed most documents and paperwork in the colonies.

THE STAMP ACT FORCES US TO PAY FOR THE ENTIRE COST OF THE WAR.

Patrick Henry was a young lawyer who spoke against the Stamp Act.

He had just finished defending townsfolk against the dishonest clergy of the Church of England. The clergy had been taking excessive payments on tobacco from the farmers.

Through his and other men's efforts, the Stamp Act was repealed.

The Stamp Act was replaced by the Townshend Acts. These laws placed a tax on imported products. Lead, paper, paint, glass, and tea were all taxed. These new laws were opposed by another notable man, Benjamin Franklin.

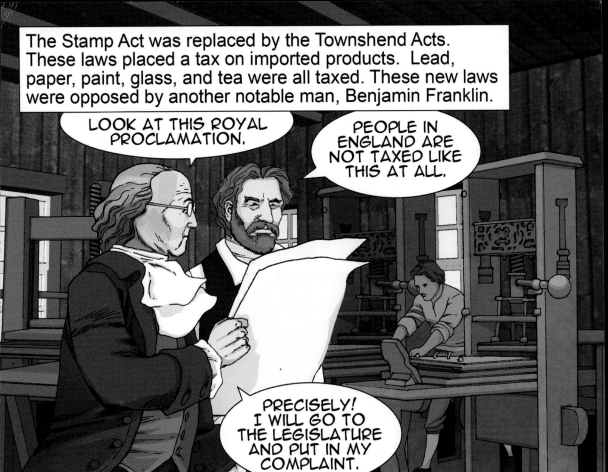

Franklin was a well-known inventor, businessman, and publisher. He wanted equal treatment for everyone.

He was known for his discoveries dealing with electricity, batteries, bifocal glasses, and stoves.

Franklin's publications included *Poor Richard's Almanack* and various other books.

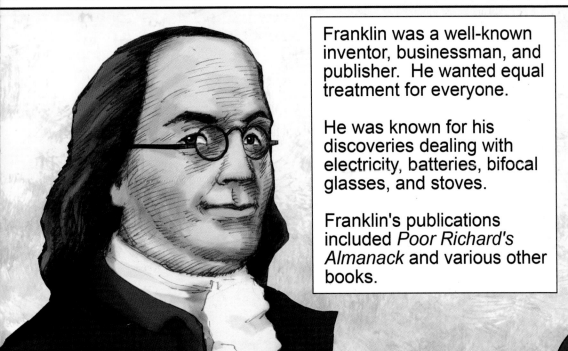

More taxes followed. The Sugar Act was one of them. Since sugar was a common need, there was widespread grumbling once again. This led Thomas Paine to write a pamphlet called *Common Sense*.

THOMAS, YOUR PAMPHLET ABOUT INDEPENDENCE COULD LAND YOU IN TROUBLE WITH THE AUTHORITIES.

THESE ARE TIMES THAT TRY MEN'S SOULS.

COMMON SENSE;

ADDRESSED TO THE

INHABITANTS

OF

AMERICA,

On the following interesting

SUBJECTS.

I. Of the Origin and Design of Government in general, with concise Remarks on the English Constitution.

II. Of Monarchy and Hereditary Succession.

III. Thoughts on the present State of American Affairs.

IV. Of the present Ability of America, with some miscellaneous Reflections.

Man knows no Master save creating HEAVEN,
Or those whom choice and common good ordain.
THOMSON.

PHILADELPHIA;

Printed, and Sold, by R. BELL, in Third-Street.

MDCCLXXVI.

Paine's pamphlet was printed on December 22, 1775. It contained a powerful argument for independence.

It said independence would bring about better trade relations with other countries. It also said that a monarchy is a terrible system to be under. Finally, it said that because of the great distance from England, the Americas should be their own country.

Common Sense spread throughout the colonies. It sold 120,000 copies.

On March 5, 1770, angry crowds confronted the British redcoats in Boston. Suddenly firing began. It was over in moments, but five men were killed in the confusion. The "Boston Massacre," as it was soon known, fanned the flames of rebellion even further.

News like this was spread by a prominent silversmith in Boston named Paul Revere.

Revere served the cause of independence by spreading news and information. He did this through his writings and by word of mouth on horseback.

Born of a Yankee mother and French father, he became one of Boston's best silversmiths.

Because of his and other men's efforts, the Townshend Acts were repealed.

15

But the tax on tea remained. The British East India Company was exempt from this tax, which angered the colonists. On December 16, 1773, 150 men and boys dressed as Native Americans. They climbed aboard three English cargo ships filled with tea and threw the crates into the harbor. This was later known as the Boston Tea Party.

On September 5, 1774, the First Continental Congress met in Philadelphia to discuss the events in Massachusetts.

The British prohibited trade in Boston. There would be no business there until the people paid for the destroyed tea.

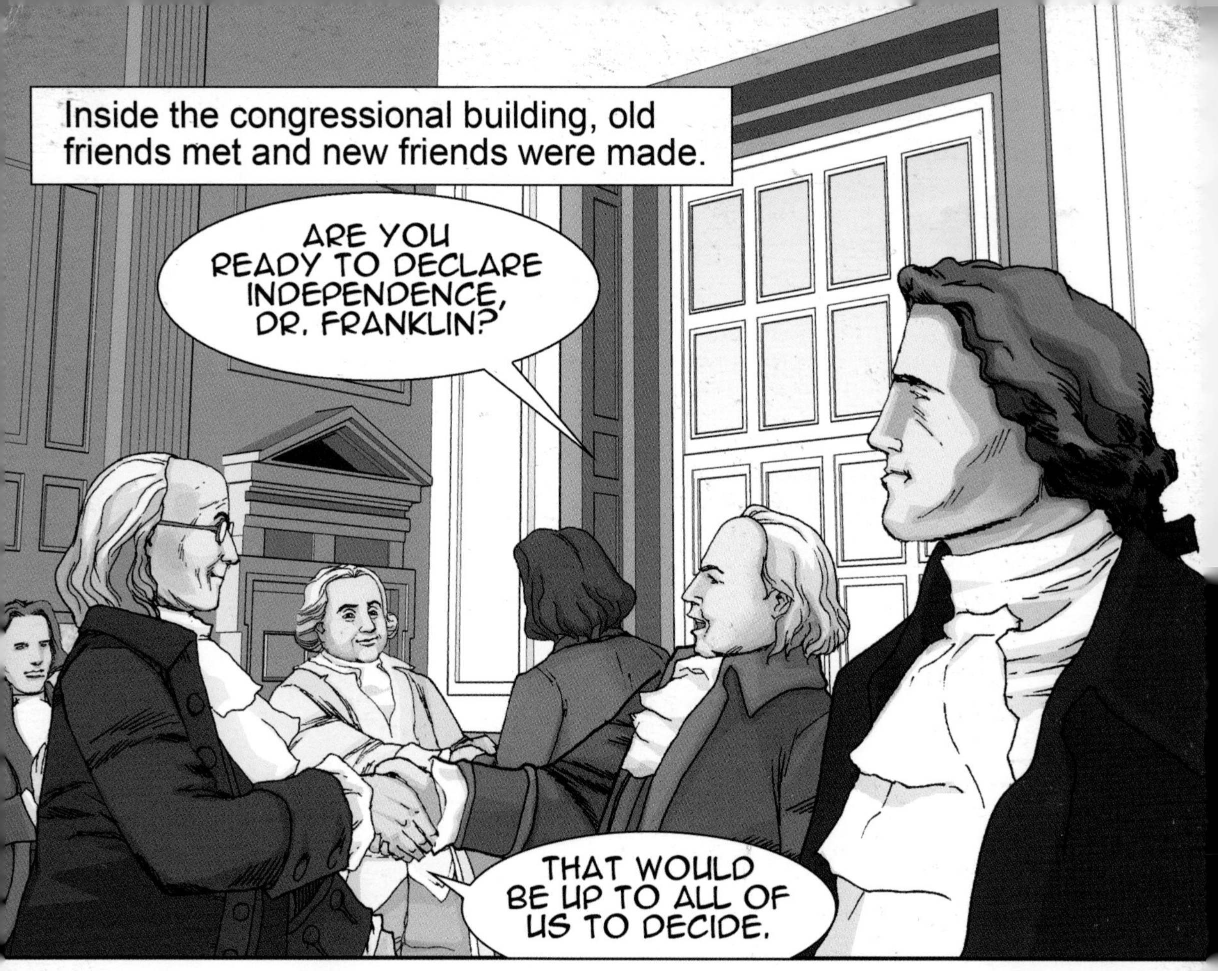
Inside the congressional building, old friends met and new friends were made.
ARE YOU READY TO DECLARE INDEPENDENCE, DR. FRANKLIN?
THAT WOULD BE UP TO ALL OF US TO DECIDE.

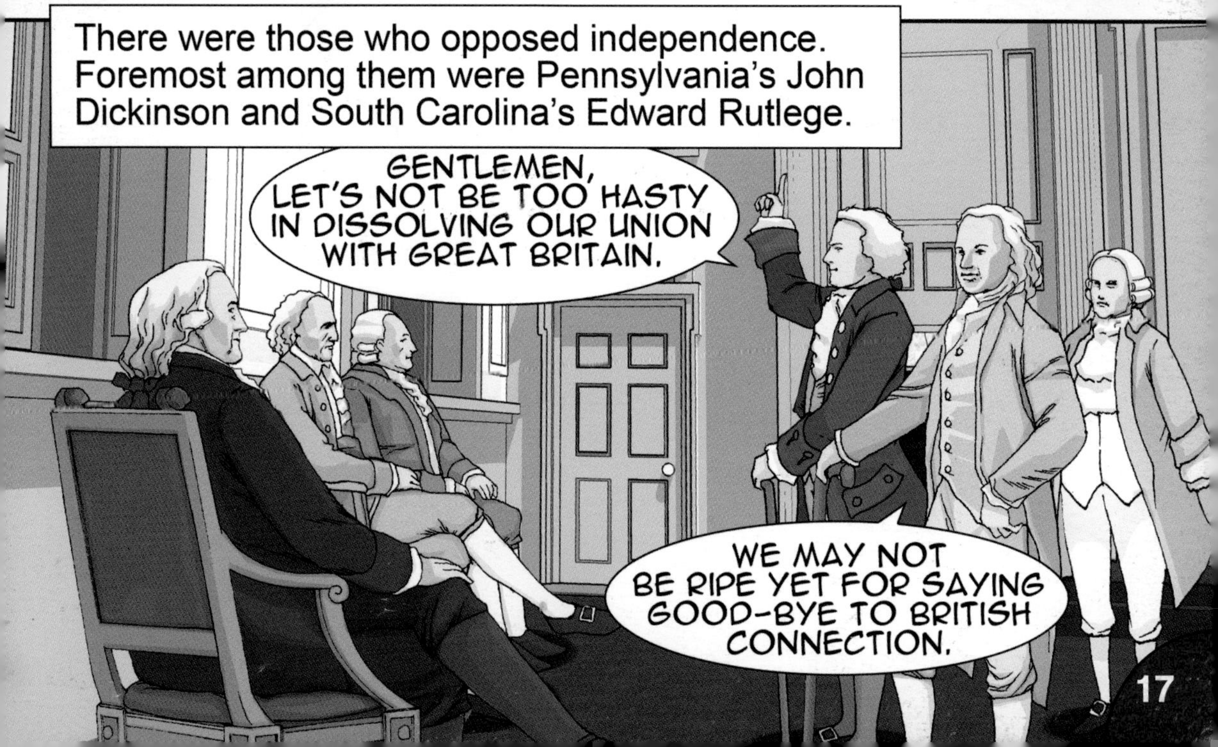
There were those who opposed independence. Foremost among them were Pennsylvania's John Dickinson and South Carolina's Edward Rutlege.
GENTLEMEN, LET'S NOT BE TOO HASTY IN DISSOLVING OUR UNION WITH GREAT BRITAIN.
WE MAY NOT BE RIPE YET FOR SAYING GOOD-BYE TO BRITISH CONNECTION.

John Adams had a difficult time convincing people to separate from England.

JOHN ADAMS, YOU'RE A TROUBLEMAKER! PENNSYLVANIA WOULD RATHER ENJOY THE BENEFITS OF BEING SUBJECTS TO ENGLAND!

WHAT BENEFITS, JOHN DICKINSON!? CRIPPLING TAXES! ABOLISHED RIGHTS!

VOTE YES FOR INDEPENDENCE!

When news of the British assault on Bunker Hill came to Congress, it was time to act.

A CONTINENTAL ARMY? WHO WOULD LEAD SUCH A RABBLE, JOHN?

NOT JUST ANY ARMY OF VOLUNTEER MILITIA, FRANKLIN. THIS WILL BE A PROFESSIONAL ARMY. AND I HAVE SOMEONE IN MIND TO NOMINATE TO BE COMMANDER IN CHIEF.

The man John Adams had in mind was a 43-year-old Virginia planter. A veteran of the French and Indian War, he was the right man to lead a young nation's army to battle.

A cause and a country also needed a flag. As legend would have it, the man who would lead the Continental army asked a seamstress to stitch one up based on his description.

The man who was nominated to lead the Continental army was George Washington. As a young man, he had led the colonial army against the French. Now, he would fight the British for the freedom of America!

Once people heard Washington would be leading the army, volunteers quickly joined the fight.

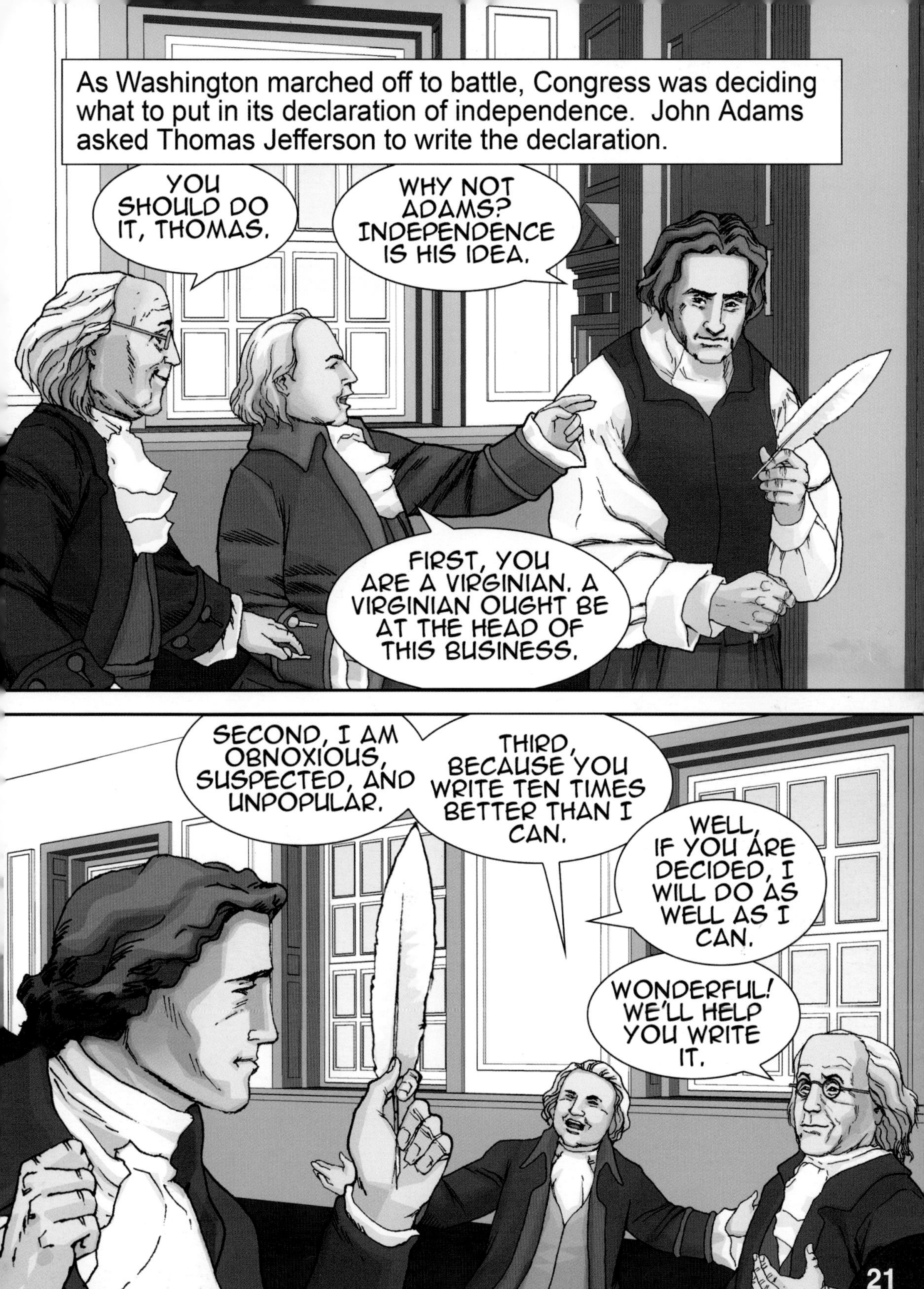
As Washington marched off to battle, Congress was deciding what to put in its declaration of independence. John Adams asked Thomas Jefferson to write the declaration.
YOU SHOULD DO IT, THOMAS.
WHY NOT ADAMS? INDEPENDENCE IS HIS IDEA.
FIRST, YOU ARE A VIRGINIAN. A VIRGINIAN OUGHT BE AT THE HEAD OF THIS BUSINESS.
SECOND, I AM OBNOXIOUS, SUSPECTED, AND UNPOPULAR.
THIRD, BECAUSE YOU WRITE TEN TIMES BETTER THAN I CAN.
WELL, IF YOU ARE DECIDED, I WILL DO AS WELL AS I CAN.
WONDERFUL! WE'LL HELP YOU WRITE IT.

While Washington was marching towards Massachusetts, the men in Philadelphia struggled with the task of declaring independence.

WHY CAN'T WE PASS THIS DECLARATION, FRANKLIN? WHAT ARE THEY ARGUING FOR?

PATIENCE, JOHN. THOSE MEN ARE NO LESS PATRIOTS OF OUR COUNTRY THAN WE ARE. WE MUST WORK WITH THEM, NOT AGAINST THEM.

During those challenging times, Adams wrote to his wife, Abigail.

MY DEAR ABIGAIL,

THANK YOU FOR ORGANIZING THE LADIES TO MAKE SALTPETER FOR GUNPOWDER. WE ARE SO CLOSE TO RATIFYING INDEPENDENCE I MUST STAY ON A BIT LONGER.

COURAGE, JOHN... ONCE THE IDEA OF INDEPENDENCE GETS AROUND, IT WILL TRAVEL FAST. WHEN FLAME IS KINDLED, LIKE LIGHTNING IT CATCHES FROM SOUL TO SOUL.

HURRY HOME, JOHN.

Chapter 6 The Hardships of Revolution

The war for independence was not going well for Washington. His men suffered terribly from the cold weather.

I HOPE THE MONEY I REQUESTED FROM CONGRESS COMES THROUGH. SOME OF MY BOYS DON'T EVEN HAVE SHOES.

On December 26, 1776, Washington led his men across the frozen Delaware River. His troops attacked the soldiers hired by England to fight the war in the Americas.

Meanwhile, Franklin went to France to ask for aid for America.

PERHAPS ENGLAND'S RIVAL CAN HELP US.

In 1780, Washington arrived at Yorktown. British troops led by Lord Cornwallis were surrounded. Their only chance was to get away by sea.

At home, the battle for independence went on!

In Trenton, New Jersey, rebels shot at the British troops from every window and barn.

HE CAN'T HOLD OUT FOR MUCH LONGER.

INDEED. LORD CORNWALLIS'S ONLY CHANCE IS ESCAPING BY SEA.

Congress, with the help of patriots such as Patrick Henry, Samuel Adams, and Paul Revere, kept the Continental army supplied as best they could.

WE'RE ALL COMMITTED NOW. INDEPENDENCE HAS BEEN DECLARED.

The French came in by sea. A fleet commanded by Admiral de Grasse defeated the British fleet.

Franklin was able to convince the French to send even more troops and supplies.

WHAT BENEFIT WILL MY COUNTRY GET IF WE HELP YOU?

WELL, YOUR HIGHNESS, WE CAN GIVE YOU SPECIAL TRADE DEALS.

IT'S ALSO AN OPPORTUNITY TO GET BACK AT YOUR RIVALS.

When they sailed away, Cornwallis was trapped at Yorktown.

Washington and his French allies defeated Cornwallis's army at Yorktown. On October 19, 1781, Cornwallis surrendered. The United States had won!

Washington wrote to Congress: "Sir: I have the honor to inform Congress, that a reduction of the British Army under the Command of Lord Cornwallis, is most happily effected."

The war for independence was over! George Washington was elected as the first president of the United States in 1789 and then again in 1793.

John Adams's vision of U.S. independence had been realized. He remained active in politics. He was elected president of the United States in 1796.

In CONGRESS, July 4, 1776.

The unanimous Declaration of the thirteen united States of America

When, in the course of human events, it becomes necessary for one people to dissolve the political bonds which have connected them with another, and to assume among the powers of the earth, the separate and equal station to which the laws of nature and of nature's God entitle them, a decent respect to the opinions of mankind requires that they should declare the causes which impel them to the separation.

We hold these truths to be self-evident, that all men are created equal, that they are endowed by their Creator with certain unalienable rights, that among these are life, liberty and the pursuit of happiness. That to secure these rights, governments are instituted among men, deriving their just powers from the consent of the governed. That whenever any form of government becomes destructive to these ends, it is the right of the people to alter or to abolish it, and to institute new government, laying its foundation on such principles and organizing its powers in such form, as to them shall seem most likely to effect their safety and happiness. Prudence, indeed, will dictate that governments long established should not be changed for light and transient causes; and accordingly all experienc hath shown that mankind are more disposed to suffer, while evils are sufferable, than to right themselves by abolishing the forms to which they are accustomed. But when a long train of abuses and usurpations, pursuing invariably the same object evinces a design to reduce them under absolute despotism, it is their right, it is their duty, to throw off such government, and to provide new guards for their future security. --Such has been the patient sufferance of these colonies; and such is now the necessity which constrains them to alter their former systems of government. The history of the present King of Great Britain is a history of repeated injuries and usurpations, all having in direct object the establishment of an absolute tyranny over these states. To prove this, let facts be submitted to a candid world.

He has refused his assent to laws, the most wholesome and necessary for the public good. He has forbidden his governors to pass laws of immediate and pressin importance, unless suspended in their operation till his assent should be obtained; and when so suspended, he has utterly neglected to attend to them. He has refused to pass other laws for the accommodation of large districts of people, unless those people would relinquish the right of representation in the legislature, right inestimable to them and formidable to tyrants only. He has called together legislative bodies at places unusual, uncomfortable, and distant from the depository of their public records, for the sole purpose of fatiguing them into compliance with his measures. He has dissolved representative houses repeatedly, for opposing with manly firmness his invasions on the rights of the people. He has refused for a long time, after such dissolutions, to cause others to be elected; whereby the legislative powers, incapable of annihilation, have returned to the people at large for their exercise; the state remaining in the meantime exposed to all the dangers of invasion from without, and convulsions within. He has endeavored to prevent the population of these states; for that purpose obstructing the laws for naturalization of foreigners; refusing to pass others to encourage their migration hither, and raising the conditions of new appropriations of lands. He has obstructed the administration of justice, by refusing his assent to laws for establishing judiciary powers. He has made judges dependent on his will alone, for the tenure of their offices, and the amount and payment of their salaries. He has erected a multitude of new offices, and sent hither swarms of officers to harass our people, and eat out their substance. He has kept among us, in times of peace, standing armies without the consent of our legislature.
He has affected to render the military independent of and superior to civil power. He has combined with others to subject us to a jurisdiction foreign to our constitution, and unacknowledged by our laws; giving his assent to their acts of pretended legislation: For quartering large bodies of armed troops among us: For protecting them, by mock trial, from punishment for any murders which they should commit on the inhabitants of these states: For cutting off our trade with all parts of the world: For imposing taxes on us without our consent: For depriving us in many cases, of the benefits of trial by jury:
For transporting us beyond seas to be tried for pretended offenses: For abolishing the free system of English laws in a neighboring province, establishing therein an arbitrary government, and enlarging its boundaries so as to render it at once an example and fit instrument for introducing the same absolute rule in these colonies: For taking away our charters, abolishing our most valuable laws, and altering fundamentally the forms of our governments: For suspending our own legislatures, and declaring themselves invested with power to legislate for us in all cases whatsoever. He has abdicated government here, by declaring us out of his protection and waging war against us. He has plundered our seas, ravaged our coasts, burned our towns, and destroyed the lives of our people. He is at this time transporting large armies of foreign mercenaries to complete the works of death, desolation and tyranny, already begun with circumstances of cruelty and perfidy scarcely paralleled in the most barbarous ages, and totally unworthy the head of a civilized nation. He has constrained our fellow citizens taken captive on the high seas to bear arms against their country, to become the executioners of their friends and brethren, or to fall themselves by their hands. He has excited domestic insurrections amongst us, and has endeavored to bring on the inhabitants of our frontiers, the merciless Indian savages, whose known rule of warfare, is undistinguished destruction of all ages, sexes and conditions. In every stage of these oppressions we have petitioned for redress in the most humble terms: our repeated petitions have been answered only by repeated injury. A prince, whose character is thus marked by every act which may define a tyrant, is unfit to be the ruler of a free people. Nor have we been wanting in attention to our British brethren. We have warned them from time to time of attempts by their legislature to extend an unwarrantable jurisdiction over us. We have reminded them of the circumstances of our emigration and settlement here. We have appealed to their native justice and magnanimity, and we have conjured them by the ties of our common kindred to disavow these usurpations, which, would inevitably interrupt our connections and correspondence. We must, therefore, acquiesce in the necessity, which denounces our separation, and hold them, as we hold the rest of mankind, enemies in war, in peace friends.

We, therefore, the representatives of the United States of America, in General Congress, assembled, appealing to the Supreme Judge of the world for the rectitude of our intentions, do, in the name, and by the authority of the good people of these colonies, solemnly publish and declare, that these united colonies are, and of right ought to be free and independent states; that they are absolved from all allegiance to the British Crown, and that all political connection between them and the state of Great Britain, is and ought to be totally dissolved; and that as free and independent states, they have full power to levy war, conclude peace, contract alliances, establish commerce, and to do all other acts and things which independent states may of right do. And for the support of this declaration, with a firm reliance on the protection of Divine Providence, we mutually pledge to each other our lives, our fortunes and our sacred honor.

John Hancock

Button Gwinnett
Lyman Hall
Geo Walton.

Wm Hooper
Joseph Hewes,
John Penn

Edward Rutledge
Thos Heyward Junr.
Thomas Lynch Junr.
Arthur Middleton

Samuel Chase
Wm Paca
Thos Stone
Charles Carroll of Carrollton

George Wythe
Richard Henry Lee
Th Jefferson
Benj Harrison
Thos Nelson jr.
Francis Lightfoot Lee
Carter Braxton

Robt Morris
Benjamin Rush
Benj. Franklin
John Morton
Geo Clymer
Jas. Smith
Geo. Taylor
James Wilson
Geo. Ross
Caesar Rodney
Geo Read
Tho M:Kean

Wm Floyd
Phil. Livingston
Frans. Lewis
Lewis Morris
Richd Stockton
Jno Witherspoon
Fras. Hopkinson
John Hart
Abra Clark

Josiah Bartlett
Wm Whipple
Saml Adams
John Adams
Robt Treat Paine
Elbridge Gerry
Step. Hopkins
William Ellery
Roger Sherman
Sam el Huntington
Wm Williams
Oliver Wolcott
Matthew Thornton

Glossary

bifocal - having one part that corrects for near vision and one for distant vision.

exempt - released from a rule or law that others must follow.

maritime - affected by the ocean, sea, or other large body of water.

oppress - to govern harshly or to keep down unjustly or cruelly.

proclamation - an official public announcement.

rebellion - an armed resistance or defiance of a government.

repeal - to formally withdraw or cancel.

unconstitutional - something that goes against the laws of a constitution.

Web Sites

To learn more about the American Revolution, visit ABDO Publishing Company on the World Wide Web at **www.abdopublishing.com.** Web sites about the American Revolution are featured on our Book Links page. These links are routinely monitored and updated to provide the most current information available.

Index

A
Adams, Abigail 22, 29
Adams, John 17, 18, 19, 21, 22, 29
Adams, Samuel 26

B
Boston Massacre 15
Boston Tea Party 16

C
Columbus, Christopher 6, 7
Continental army 18, 19, 20, 26
Continental Congress 16, 17, 18, 21, 23, 26, 28
Cornwallis, Charles 24, 25, 27, 28

D
de Grasse (admiral) 26
Dickinson, John 17, 18

F
France 7, 8, 9, 10, 20, 24, 26, 27, 28
Franklin, Benjamin 13, 17, 18, 22, 24, 27
French and Indian War 10, 11, 12, 19

G
George (king of England) 8, 9

H
Henry, Patrick 12, 26

J
Jefferson, Thomas 21

M
Marquis of Montcalm 11

N
Native Americans 9, 10, 16

P
Paine, Thomas 14
Paris, Treaty of 10

R
Revere, Paul 15, 26
Ross, Betsy 19
Rutlege, Edward 17

S
Spain 6, 7

T
taxes 12, 13, 14, 15, 16, 18
trade 8, 11, 14, 16, 27

W
Washington, George 19, 20, 21, 22, 23, 24, 28
Wolfe, James 11

Celebrity Entrepreneurs

RIHANNA

Katie Griffiths

Cavendish
Square

New York

Published in 2015 by Cavendish Square Publishing, LLC
243 5th Avenue, Suite 136, New York, NY 10016

Copyright © 2015 by Cavendish Square Publishing, LLC

First Edition

CPSIA Compliance Information: Batch #WW15CSQ

All websites were available and accurate when this book was sent to press.

Library of Congress Cataloging-in-Publication Data

Griffiths, Katie.
Rihanna / Katie Griffiths.
pages cm. — (Celebrity entrepreneurs)
Includes index.
ISBN 978-1-50260-029-5 (hardcover) ISBN 978-1-50260-030-1 (paperback) ISBN 978-1-50260-031-8 (ebook)
1. Rihanna, 1988— -Juvenile literature. 2. Singers—Biography—Juvenile literature. I. Title.

ML3930.R44G75 2015
782.42164092—dc23
[B]

2014024957

Editor: Kristen Susienka
Copy Editor: Cynthia Roby
Art Director: Jeffrey Talbot
Designer: Joseph Macri
Senior Production Manager: Jennifer Ryder-Talbot
Production Editor: David McNamara
Photo Researcher: J8 Media

The photographs in this book are used by permission and through the courtesy of: Cover photo by Kevin Mazur/Getty Images; Frederick M. Brown/Getty Images, 4; PRNewsFoto/Parlux Fragrances LTD, 9; Rob Verhorst/Redferns/Getty Images, 10; Anton_Ivanov/Shutterstock.com, 12; Everett Collection/Shutterstock.com, 13; Sasha/Hulton Archive/Getty Images, 15; NC1 WENN Photos/Newscom, 18; Everett Collection/Shutterstock.com, 20; Press Association via AP Images, 21; BERTRAND GUAY/AFP/Getty Images/Newscom, 22; FREDERIC J. BROWN/AFP/Getty Images, 26; Kevin Winter/Getty Images, 28; Larry Busacca/Getty Images, 30; Kevin Winter/Getty Images, 32; KARIM SAHIB/AFP/Getty Images, 33; Ilikeriri/File:Rihanna Cologne 2013 03 (Edited).png/Wikimedia Commons, 34; Everett Collection/Shutterstock.com, 37; infch-02/INFphoto.com/Newscom, 39.

Printed in the United States of America

CONTENTS

INTRODUCTION Rihanna Shining Bright   5

CHAPTER ONE Climbing the Ladder   11

CHAPTER TWO Building a Brand   19

CHAPTER THREE Brand Success   27

CHAPTER FOUR Looking to the Future   35

CAREER HIGHLIGHTS TIMELIME   42

GLOSSARY   43

FURTHER INFORMATION   45

INDEX   47

ABOUT THE AUTHOR   48

Rihanna is on top of the world—but how did she get there?

Rihanna Shining Bright

The world has many celebrities. Some are actors, some are singers, and some dedicate their lives to many different industries. In a world that constantly changes, more celebrities are becoming **entrepreneurs**. This allows them to alter the face of fashion, design, and beauty. How did they do this? Each person has his or her own story of how they got to where they are today. You don't have to be a celebrity to be successful, however. Anyone can be an entrepreneur with hard work, determination, and imagination.

Beginnings

In 2003, a sixteen-year-old girl from the parish of Saint Michael in Barbados met a music producer from New York. She sang for him with her two school friends. He was so impressed that he invited her to come and work with him in New York. The man's name was Evan Rogers. The girl's name was Robyn Fenty, or as you might know her, Rihanna.

Over the next decade or so, Rihanna became known all over the world for her voice. However, she was interested in more than singing. Soon she moved from music into new industries, such as fashion, perfume, television, and movies. She found success time and time again in each of these areas, but how and when did she start?

Perfumes

Rihanna began expanding her **brand** in 2011. In January of that year she released her first perfume, Reb'l Fleur. Rihanna said she chose the name because "my grandmother in Barbados used to call me her Rebel Flower." The popular fragrance was sold at Macy's. Rihanna was able to tell her fans about the new perfume quickly by using social media. She posted a one-minute video to her then 34 million Twitter and Facebook followers. By the end of the year, the perfume had made $80 million in-store.

Critics loved her perfume. A critic is a person who tells people how good or bad something is.

One critic said if Rihanna kept selling "scents this good, [she would] have a new favorite in the celebrity scent department."

Fashion

It was also in 2011 that Rihanna worked with the Italian fashion designer Giorgio Armani and introduced her first fashion line. She designed clothes for both Armani Jeans and Emporio Armani Underwear. Armani was pleased with Rihanna's ideas. He described Rihanna as "a great artist. Her personality, charisma, and energy made it a pleasure to work with her." The collection was also highly praised by many fashion critics.

Makeup

Rihanna didn't stop at fashion and fragrances. At the beginning of 2013, she teamed with MAC Cosmetics and began a new business venture, the RiRi Hearts MAC Collection. This collection was to be four seasonal makeup lines released at different times during the year. The deal was groundbreaking. Rihanna was not just a model for the makeup but also a designing partner. This meant she could choose colors, packaging, and how the makeup would look. It was the first time that MAC had worked with a celebrity on more than one line.

Jennifer Balbier, one of MAC's senior vice presidents, explained why Rihanna was different. "She's a star," said Balbier. "The world follows her look—how she wears her hair, her nails, her clothing, how she styles herself."

Rihanna showed herself again to be as talented at designing as she was at singing. "When it comes to creating things, I like to get my hands in there," she says.

Media

Many **public relations (PR)** professionals use Rihanna as an example of excellent social media marketing. Rihanna now has more than 28 million Twitter followers and 66 million Facebook fans. She regularly updates her Twitter, Facebook, Instagram, YouTube, and Google+ accounts. She shares personal photos and thoughts, and gives fans the latest news, events, and images from her music and business projects. All this keeps her in the public eye. It also helps her to advertise her albums and other products for free.

Expressing Herself

A fashion designer, perfume creator, makeup artist, and global superstar, Rihanna has many different talents. Why did she want to be more than a singer, though? "Being creative is something that I love," she says. "I can put that [creativity] into different [things]." She also said that creating products was not very different from making songs. "My makeup looks, my fashion looks … they help me to express myself as an artist."

Rihanna has moved from the music world into other industries. These other areas have allowed her to tap into her creative freedom. Rihanna is more than an artist, she is a business. So how did she achieve this empire? How did she recreate herself as a brand? What does this mean for future female celebrities?

Rihanna's perfumes are just one way she expresses her creativity.

All the way from Saint Michael to New York City.

Chapter One

Climbing the Ladder

Robyn Rihanna Fenty was born one of three children on February 20, 1988. She lived in a three-bedroom bungalow in the parish of Saint Michael, Barbados. Her mother is a retired accountant, and her father is a warehouse supervisor. She has two brothers, Rorrey and Rajad. She also has two half sisters and a half brother from her father's side. A young entrepreneur, Rihanna sold clothes at her father's street stall.

Rihanna's childhood was very difficult. Her father struggled with drug and alcohol addiction. Her parents' marriage ended when she was just fourteen. She escaped her pain through music and started singing at the age of seven. Her inspirations include Alicia Keys, Madonna,

Mariah Carey, Janet Jackson, Gwen Stefani, Bob Marley, and Brandy Norwood. By the time she reached high school, she had formed a music group with two classmates.

Rihanna's childhood parish of Saint Michael.

A Big Break

In December 2003, fifteen-year-old Rihanna met music producer Evan Rogers, who had come to Barbados on vacation. He had heard about Rihanna through mutual friends and invited her and her two classmates for an audition at his hotel. Rogers was very impressed with her voice. He invited Rihanna and her mother to his home in Connecticut to record some **demo** tapes. Soon after, she was signed to Rogers' production company, SRP Productions.

At the end of 2004, Rihanna's demo tape was sent to several recording labels. One of these was Def Jam Recordings. An executive there found Rihanna's tape and played it for Jay-Z, the label's then-president and **CEO**. Impressed by what he heard, Jay-Z invited Rihanna to New York City to audition for the label. Rihanna traveled to New York in February 2005. After hearing her sing three songs, Jay-Z signed her on the spot for a six-album deal. "I signed her in one day," Jay-Z told *Rolling Stone*. "It took me two minutes to see she was a star."

Rihanna with mentor, Jay-Z.

The Jump to Stardom

Rihanna's debut single, "Pon de Replay," was released three months later, reaching the top five on music charts in fifteen countries. The single was quickly followed by her debut album, *Music of the Sun*, which sold over two million copies worldwide. A month after its release Rihanna was already working on her second album, *A Girl Like Me*. It had even greater success than her first, selling 115,000 copies in its first week. Initially, critics were not impressed with Rihanna's music. *Rolling Stone* rated her first album only two and a half out of five stars, arguing that it "lacks the single's immediacy and rhythmic **ingenuity**."

Despite criticism, Rihanna carried on and worked even harder. Things changed in 2007 when Rihanna released her third album, *Good Girl Gone Bad*. The songs were more up-tempo and had dance tracks underneath the melodies. With these new songs, she had a string of hits.

Rihanna has since made four more albums, won six Grammy awards, sold millions of records worldwide, and made music chart history again and again. So what made her decide to try something new?

Celebrity Perfumes: A History

Celebrity perfumes have been around for nearly a hundred years. The very first was created in the 1930s. Italian fashion designer Elsa Schiaparelli designed the scent's

Elsa Schiaparelli, the godmother of celebrity perfumes.

bottle, which had an hourglass figure modeled after the dummy she used when creating actress Mae West's *Every Day's a Holiday* costumes. Since then, many actors and singers have endorsed different designer fragrances. They include Elvis Presley, Elizabeth Taylor, Marilyn Monroe, and Nicole Kidman. However, in the 1980s everything changed. Stars began to design their own perfumes. The first was Linda Evans's Forever Krystle. Since then, the number of celebrity scents has grown. Between 2002 and 2012, the industry saw the biggest change. In one decade, the number of celebrity perfumes rose from ten to over eighty. Celebrity fragrances are now worth $1.3 billion a year. They are a huge part of the United States' $5.2 billion perfume industry.

Branching Out

Rihanna landed her first **endorsement** deal in October 2005 with Secret Body Spray. She began creating beauty products in 2009. Jay-Z, the Def Jam CEO, signed a deal with Parlux Fragrances. This contract was to help launch scents for both Rihanna and Kanye West, who were artists with the label. When the perfume designers first met Rihanna, they noticed that she was wearing a "unique scent." Rihanna explained that she had made it herself. She did this by mixing and layering five different perfumes. Designers studied the five fragrances to help them create the final formula. The perfume was named Reb'l Fleur. Rihanna released the scent in January 2011, explaining that she chose perfume because she "wanted something that said, 'Rihanna was here.'" Over the next four years Rihanna introduced three more perfumes: Rebelle, Nude, and Rogue.

Rihanna's next beauty venture was with makeup. In 2013, she worked with MAC Cosmetics to create four makeup lines. There was one for summer, one for spring, and two holiday collections. They were known as the RiRi Hearts MAC collections. MAC Cosmetics was an easy choice for Rihanna. "I have always loved makeup," she said. "I always said that if I do it, I want to do it with a credible brand."

Rihanna then moved to the fashion industry. In November 2011, she designed her first line for Armani. Small lines such as this are called capsule collections. The designs, an interesting mix of casual and rock, gave her fans the opportunity to dress like their favorite star.

The Story of Celebrity Fashion Lines

Gianni Versace was the first designer to bring celebrities into the fashion world. He loved **pop culture** and decided to give celebrities front-row seats at his fashion shows. Why did he use celebrities?

In 1989 and 1992, two important events took place. In 1989, the Internet was invented. In 1992, a woman named Fern Mallis introduced the first New York Fashion Week. Together, these two events changed the fashion industry forever. Designers needed to get lots of attention for their labels; otherwise they could not become successful. If celebrities came to see their shows, several reporters would follow them, take photos, and sell them to magazines. The magazines would then publish the photos and the designer would get free publicity. Soon celebrities wanted more than just a seat. They began designing their own clothing lines, and celebrity fashion became a valuable business.

W

Rated XX: Women
Directors Crack
Hollywood's A-List

Beyond Gloss:
Lipstick Makes
A Comeback

Also: The Bright
Young Ingenue of
Alice in Wonderland
& London's Exclusive
New Private Club

THE **POP**
PRINCESS
PROVES
LOOKING HO
IS THE BEST
REVENGE

RIHANNA

Rihanna uses her
image to promote
her own style.

Chapter Two

Building a Brand

What is a brand? A brand is a name of a product or a **manufacturer**. It is a very important part of selling. If you don't have a good brand, people may not want to buy from you. What is Rihanna's brand? In a word: Rihanna. Her brand is designed around her personal style and attitude. She uses this image to sell products. What kind of products has she made? What do they say about her brand?

Sassy Scents

Parlux Fragrances manufactured Rihanna's first perfume, Reb'l Fleur. Their idea was to create something that reflected Rihanna's personality. They began by exploring the five fragrances Rihanna had mixed together that blended sweet and bitter, making her own "unique scent."

A Canopy of Cash: Rihanna and Totes

In 2009, Rihanna released her smash hit "Umbrella." It caught the attention of marketing executives at Totes Isotoner, an umbrella company. The company had been making umbrellas for more than thirty years but had not used a celebrity

Under a Totes Isotoner umbrella.

endorsement for almost a decade. Because Rihanna's song was catchy, Totes knew that it could be useful for them to get her involved with their company. Rihanna agreed, and was signed immediately as spokesperson.

Totes and her "Umbrella" song were a good fit, but Rihanna's brand was all about being cool. Any product she endorsed needed tocontribute to her image. To make this happen, Rihanna also helped Totes create customized umbrellas. She took part in designing ones with sparkly fabrics and glittery charms on the handles.

Eventually, the perfume Parlux Fragrances would create was a mix of tuberose, violet, hibiscus, and coconut water. The bottle would also be part of her brand and had to reflect her personality. Because Rihanna loved wearing heels, they created a special bottle to look like the heel of a high-heeled shoe.

The fragrance was advertised as something both sweet and playful. Its promotional video showed Rihanna walking through a walled garden. While the song played, her image changed from a sweet girl in pink to a rebel girl in black. British newspapers praised the video for "showing off [Rihanna's] saucy and innocent sides." By the end of 2011, it was clear the perfume was successful, making $80 million in sales.

Rihanna with the heel-inspired fragrance bottle for Reb'l Fleur.

Rock Star Labels

Rihanna's personality can also be seen in her fashion products. The **initial concept** of her line with Armani was to create clothing in Rihanna's style: glamorous with a rock edge. She helped to design a limited edition collection for Armani's line of jeans and underwear. About her personal style, Rihanna says, "I don't usually like typical … girly-girly stuff … I always like something that's … not typical or expected." The designers used this information to build the collection. The final result was biker jackets, trendy jeans, leather bags, underwear, and T-shirts. The line reflected Rihanna's dislike of "girly-girly" looks.

Rihanna brings her own style to every fashion venture.

What Makes a Good Brand?

1. The Right Customer

To create a good brand, you must know who you want to buy your product. How old are they? What do they like? What do they want to be? Knowing this helps you to decide what to sell. So who are Rihanna's customers? They are people who like her music, style, and attitude, and want her celebrity lifestyle. They are probably young and adventurous.

2. Personality

If a person is fun and has a happy personality, you will like him. If a person is rude or untrustworthy, you will not like them. A brand personality is used to attract the right customer. Rihanna's right customer is young, adventurous, and loves fashion. Her brand personality is about being stylish, confident, and successful, which is perfect for keeping her customers and fans happy.

3. Quality Products

Personality and the right customer only go so far. If a company sells bad products, they will quickly be known for poor quality. Rihanna makes high-quality products. She always works with companies with reputations for quality. Armani, River Island, and MAC, for example, all have a good product history.

Rihanna continued to use her tough but stylish look for her other clothing lines. In 2013, she released her first collection with the British store River Island. The line was later presented at London Fashion Week.

Perfect Pouts

Rihanna is also well known for bold and trendsetting looks in makeup. This reputation was important in selling her third product, RiRi Hearts MAC. In 2013, Rihanna signed a deal with MAC. Together they made lines of summer, fall, and holiday makeup. A MAC representative said it was a combination of "pop culture, fast fashion, and iconic style and makeup."

Rihanna was very involved in the makeup's creation. She selected packaging, colors, makeup textures, and finishes. Her signature was put on the packaging. It was also embossed onto blush and eye shadow palettes. She made her own personal red lipstick, the RiRi Woo, based on the company's most famous lipstick, the Ruby Woo. This was a clever business decision for Rihanna, who had made something unique that her fans would want.

Rihanna's first makeup line became available in May 2013. She used her own social media to advertise. She tweeted, "That's right baby, I'm a #MACgirl now!" She also added pictures of the newly packaged cosmetics. MAC gave fans another preview. They set up pop-up shops at Rihanna's tour shows. This allowed fans to buy samples before they hit stores.

The Rihanna Brand

What is Rihanna's brand? Rihanna's brand is her lifestyle. It is her fashion and her attitude. It is an image of being fun, stylish, and rebellious. It attracts customers who want this kind of life. She chooses products that help this image. Her products help customers to create a version of her life. Her clothing lines and makeup are lifestyle accessories for her fans. They are fun, flirty, and created in Rihanna's image.

Rihanna at the
Grammy Awards
ceremony in 2013.

Chapter Three

Brand Success

How successful is Rihanna's brand? To judge this, you must keep in mind what she is selling: records and tour tickets. She also has branded products: perfumes, makeup, and clothes. Her brand sells more than items, it also sells ideas. Her clothing and makeup lines are based on her personal style. Her perfumes are made from her own individual recipes. Fans can buy a bit of Rihanna's glamour when they purchase these products.

Sales and Awards

There is one way to see Rihanna's success: you can look at her sales and awards. Rihanna's products have strong sales numbers. Reb'l Fleur, for example, made $80 million by the end of 2011.

Rebelle, her second fragrance, had sold 4 million bottles in the United Kingdom at the end of 2012. Her clothing lines with River Island were not only profitable but also raised the store's profile. Her collaboration with MAC Cosmetics was unique. MAC had never signed a deal to create more than one product with a celebrity. Where Rihanna was named a "creative partner," other celebrities with MAC had only been called "collaborators." This shows her importance to the design process.

A successful brand can collaborate with other famous brands. Brands do this for one reason: when they can both get something from the deal. Rihanna's brand brings style and fame

And the awards just keep on coming…

Rihanna "hearts" Quality

A big part of brand success is reputation. If a company sells products of poor quality, customers will remember and not buy from them in the future. The word will spread and eventually hurt the company's reputation. Rihanna's products are always high quality. The companies she works with all have reputations for making trustworthy products. She often points this out in interviews. About her decision to choose MAC when designing her makeup, Rihanna said, "When you think of makeup, the brand that pops into your mind—for something legit—is MAC."

to a product. The companies she works with must also add value. Rihanna has worked with **prestigious** brands such as Balmain fashion, MAC, and even Armani. Their willingness to work with Rihanna shows confidence in her brand. They know that her name will sell their products.

A big part of Rihanna's brand is her personality. For her brand to be successful she must be seen as cool and iconic. You can judge her image from the non-music awards she receives. In 2012, *Time* magazine put Rihanna on their 100 Most Influential People list. *Forbes* magazine ranked her fourth in their Most Powerful Celebrities list. In 2013, Rihanna was named Most Influential Celebrity on the Internet, according to the Top 50 Most Influential Celebrities, a study that was conducted by Zimbio entertainment news. What she wears one day can spark a new fashion trend the next. Many people would want to buy a product with Rihanna's name on it.

Rihanna choosing her words carefully at the Women of the Year Awards in 2009.

It's All in the Lyrics

Rihanna's products have been a big part of her brand's success. Her main product is music. She does not separate her music from her other products. She brings them all together for better sales.

Rihanna often mentions her products in her songs. In "Pour It Up," she sings, "My fragrance on and they love my smell." Talking about her perfume is a great way to promote it. She describes it as part of her celebrity life. Fans can listen to the song while wearing her perfume. People who don't have the perfume might want to buy it. Either way, the fragrance can be worn to put a little bit of Rihanna-glamour in your life.

Rihanna also uses her music to promote her brand personality. Her songs are about being a strong female. They have a clear message for girls to be tough and successful in business. In "Run

Rihanna's Rewards

To continue her success and keep her brand alive, Rihanna remains true to her first industry, music. To date, she has won twenty-two awards at the Billboard Music Awards alone, eight awards from American Music Awards, and seven Grammy awards. This includes the first ever Icon Award. This is given to an artist whose work has had "a profound influence over pop music on a global level." She was named Woman of the Year at the 2009 Glamour Magazine Women of the Year Awards. She is the only female artist ever to win two Video of the Year Awards at the MTV Video Awards. She won Most Played Artist on British Radio in both 2008 and 2012. In total, she has won 250 awards from 540 nominations.

Rihanna and Jay-Z win Best Rap/Sung Collaboration at the 52nd Grammy Awards.

This Town," Rihanna says, "Victory's within a mile / Almost there, don't give up now." She tells people to be strong and to achieve their goals. In "Pour It Up," she points out her business contacts: "Call J up and close a deal." Here she is showing herself as a go-getting businesswoman who can complete a business deal with just one phone call. These lyrics create the image of her brand. She shows herself as a strong female leader. She makes herself both glamorous and businesslike. Rihanna uses this image when selling her products, which are created for people who want her lifestyle.

To the Next Generation

What effect has Rihanna had on young girls? Has she helped them? Is she a good role model? The answers are yes, yes, and yes!

About Rihanna's influence on young girls, British artist Damien Hirst says, "Rihanna's strong and she's making a generation of women strong. She's an unlikely role model, yet hugely successful." Rihanna is sometimes a controversial figure. Some people do not like things she says or the way she dresses, but there is one thing that makes Rihanna a good role model: her business sense. She is a strong, independent businesswoman. She is creative and dynamic. Her collaborations in business and music have all been interesting and successful. She is always trying new things. She refuses to stick to only one industry. She encourages girls to be tough and determined. She teaches them not to be embarrassed to show their intelligence and ambition. She has made her name into an empire.

Rihanna's strength and energy can be seen in her performances.

Rihanna keeps her work diverse and relevant.

Chapter Four

Looking to the Future

Rihanna has achieved her empire. How did she make herself into a brand? Why has she been so successful? It's all thanks to three key tactics, which are **diversification**, brand personality, and social media.

Diversification means her brand sells more than just one thing. She has moved from music to fashion, fragrances, and makeup. She is involved with outside projects in media and television. This gives Rihanna lots of different ways to make a profit. It also keeps her relevant. People don't just have to listen to an mp3 player. They can see her on YouTube, in stores, and on television.

Brand personality is the "face" of the product. Rihanna has created an image using her personality. This image is used to sell her products. Her brand image is the "Rihanna" lifestyle—stylish, rebellious, and fun. Critics and fans alike view her as a style icon. Magazines are always interested in what she is going to say next. This is useful in two ways. First, companies know that her image will sell products. This makes them more likely to offer her business deals to represent them. Second, her look is something people want to follow, or imitate. People can channel her attitude by wearing her makeup, clothes, and fragrances, all the while listening to her music.

The role social media plays today is huge. Rihanna has cleverly used her different platforms to remain in the public eye. She has a clear idea of who her audience is. All of her activities are created to keep them interested in what she is doing. She has several pages dedicated to her fashion, music, and personal life. She uses Twitter and Instagram to connect with her fans. She has used them to express her mourning over the death of her grandmother, and confirm rumors about her love life. However, she makes use of them to promote new products as well. This means her fans are always interested in her updates. It also means that they are more willing to promote Rihanna themselves. They can retweet her Twitter messages, "like" or "favorite" her Facebook photos, and pass them on to friends. This free advertising is valuable to any celebrity. Rihanna's active fan base is also another reason for her successful business deals. Any company who works with Rihanna knows that they will have an army of Rihanna fans to help promote their product.

Lessons for the Future

What can we learn from Rihanna's success? What can her career tell us about the future of celebrity entrepreneurs? What lessons can she teach aspiring young girls? Here are three lessons to take to heart.

All smiles at the American Music Awards in 2009.

1. Be Unique, Take Risks

If every one of your friends wore the same coat to school, would you want to wear it? Probably not. You would want something different and fashionable that would reflect your personality. The same goes for celebrities. If everyone looked and dressed the same it would be a boring world. We love people and things that stand out. Rihanna has made her career on being unique. She uses her fashion, music, and hair to make big statements, ones that keep her in the public eye. Even if you aren't a Rihanna fan you will have seen her in magazines, on your Twitter feed, or heard her music on the radio. Her uniqueness makes her interesting and exciting. It makes companies want to work with her. This helps her brand succeed in different industries.

There is no mistaking that Rihanna is an individual. This has led some to label her a rebel. "I don't go out of my way to be a rebel or to have that perception," she told *Vogue*. "A lot of the decisions I make, the direction I want to move, is against the grain, and I'm aware of that sometimes … You will never be stylish if you don't take risks."

Signing posters at the opening of a MAC store in Hong Kong in 2013.

2. Partnerships Are Important

In life, we are often the sum of our friends. Good friends can help you become a better person. Bad friends can force you into negative situations. It is the same in business. As a brand the companies who you work with are important. A well-known company can give your brand more **credibility**. This can make you appear more trustworthy and thereby attract more customers. A company with bad products or a negative image can ruin your brand's credibility. Rihanna knows this very well. She only creates products with credible companies. Her history of collaboration includes deals with Nike, Clinique, and Oprah. This is in addition to her own product lines with Armani, River Island, and MAC. She has frequently pointed out her focus on quality and only chooses the best companies to work with her.

3. Personal Brands Need Social Media

Nowadays, most of the world has access to a computer. On average, people get more information from the web than from books. With social media, fans have greater access to their favorite stars. This is something celebrities have had to learn quickly. Rihanna is seen as a model for social media branding. She has created a loyal group of followers and sponsors. She has built a relationship with her fans using her Twitter and Instagram feeds. This personal branding has inspired her fans to promote her. They create different websites, blogs, and social media feeds. They discuss, promote, and forward on information about her. This helps news about her current and future products to travel quickly.

The Last Word

Through Rihanna's career you can see the future of celebrity entrepreneurs. No longer just singers, they can become powerful businesswomen. It is not an easy path, but their lessons can be applied to any future career. Be strong. Be ambitious. Learn a variety of skills. The more you learn, the more successful you will be. Last, and most importantly, push yourself and stand out.

Career Highlights Timeline

2003	Rihanna is discovered
2004	Signs to Def Jam Recordings
2005	First single released
2006	Signs her first endorsement deal with Secret Body Spray; releases *Music of the Sun*; reaches number one with "SOS"
2006	Tops the *Billboard* Year-End Charts as the Top Pop Female Artist, Top Hot 100 Singles Female Artist, Top Pop 100 Artist
2007	Releases *Good Girl Gone Bad*
2009	Release of *Rated R*; named Top Digital Song Artist of the Decade at the *Billboard* Music Awards; signs with Parlux Fragrances to begin perfume line
2011	Releases her first perfume, Reb'l Fleur; collaborates with Armani to release her first capsule clothing collection; opens 2011 Billboard Music Awards
2013	Teams up with MAC Cosmetics; receives first ever Icon Award at the American Music Awards

Glossary

brand The process involved in creating a unique name and image for a product in the consumers' mind, mainly through advertising campaigns with a consistent theme.

CEO Chief executive officer; a person who holds the highest position in a company. The CEO has the overall responsibility for a company's day-to-day workings.

credibility The ability to inspire belief or trust.

demo A recording intended to show off a song or performer to a record producer.

diversification When a company or organization goes into new areas of business.

endorsement When a person or company gives official approval of something, such as a new product.

entrepreneur A person who organizes, owns, manages, and assumes the risks of a business; a businessperson.

ingenuity Cleverness and originality.

initial concept The first idea. Usually what a company first wants the product to be, before it has been made.

manufacturer One who changes the form of a product or who creates a new product.

pop culture Short for "popular culture." This includes music, TV shows, and products that are made for the general population.

prestigious When something has an impressive or important reputation.

public relations (PR) A strategic communication process that builds mutually beneficial relationships between organizations or individuals and their public.

Further Information

Books

Govan, Chloe. *Rihanna: Rebel Flower*. London, England: Omnibus Press, 2012.

Henwood, Simon. *Rihanna*. New York, NY: Rizzoli, 2010.

Krumenauer, Heidi. *Rihanna*. Blue Banner Biographies. Hockessin, DE: Mitchel Lane Publishers, 2008.

White, Danny. *Rihanna: The Unauthorized Biography*. London, England: Michael O'Mara Books Limited, 2013.

Websites

Forbes Profile: Rihanna
www.forbes.com/profile/rihanna
This in-depth profile on the star's business and entertainment deals with detailed information on her earnings, wealth ranking, and net worth.

Rihanna Daily

www.rihannadaily.com

Extensive Rihanna fan site with a wealth of information on her current and past activities. It includes a large imag archive with connections to various fan forums.

Rihanna Now

www.rihannanow.com/rihanna-now

Check out Rihanna's official website, which features news, tour dates, videos, photos, lyrics, her biography, and relevant press releases.

Videos

Rihanna—Half of Me Documentary (2013)

www.youtube.com/
watch?v=yC5yNqnp6Ag&list=RDyC5yNqnp6Ag

This video features interviews with Rihanna and her fans discussing Rihanna's persona and how she connects with her fan base.

Rihanna—Road To 'Talk That Talk' (Part 1)

www.youtube.com/watch?v=y432iwEl_Z4

Watch documentary footage from the making of her album *Talk That Talk* and her Loud tour.

Index

Page numbers in **boldface** are illustrations.

Armani, 7, 17, 22, 23, 29, 40
Armani, Giorgio, 7

Balmain fashion, 29
brand personality, 23, 31,
    35–36

Clinique, 40

Def Jam Recordings, 13, 16
diversification, 35

Hirst, Damien, 33

Jay-Z, **13**, 16, **32**

MAC Cosmetics, 7–8, 16–17,
    23, 24–25, 28, 29, **39**, 40
    RiRi Hearts MAC
        Collection, 7, 16, 24
    RiRi Woo, 24

Nike, 40

Parlux Fragrances, 16, 19, 21

Rihanna,
    and social media, 6, 8,
        24–25, 35, 36, 40–41
    awards, 14, **26**, 27–30, 31,
        32, **37**
    early music career, 5–6,
        11–14
    family, 11
        Fentyn, Robyn
            Rihanna, 11–12
    lyrics, 30–32
    perfume brands,
        Nude, 16
        Reb'l Fleur, 6–7, 16,
            19, **21**, 27
        Rebelle, 16, 28
        Rogue, **9**, 16
    River Island, 23, 24, 28, 40
    Rogers, Evan, 6, 12–13

Saint Michael, Barbados, 5–6,
    10, 11–12
Schiaparelli, Elsa, **15**

Totes Isotoner, 20

Versace, Gianni, 17

About the Author

Katie Griffiths is a freelance author and communications consultant with a strong background in pop culture, marketing, and social media. For more information, visit katiegriffiths. net.